Releasing the Burden of SHAME

Charles R. Swindoll

INSIGHT FOR LIVING

RELEASING THE BURDEN OF SHAME

By Charles R. Swindoll

Charles R. Swindoll has devoted his life to the clear, practical teaching and application of God's Word and His grace. Chuck currently is the senior pastor of Stonebriar Community Church in Frisco, Texas, but his listening audience extends far beyond this local church body. As a leading program in Christian broadcasting, *Insight for Living* airs in major Christian radio markets around the world, reaching people groups in languages they can understand. Chuck's extensive writing ministry has also served the body of Christ worldwide, and his leadership as president and now chancellor of Dallas Theological Seminary has helped prepare and equip a new generation for ministry.

Published By:
IFL Publishing House
A Division of Insight for Living
Post Office Box 251007
Plano, Texas 75025-1007

The text of this booklet was taken from chapter 4 "Getting Through the Tough Stuff of Shame" of Charles R. Swindoll's book *Getting Through the Tough Stuff: It's Always Something!* (Nashville: W Publishing Group, 2004) 47–60. Copyright © 2004 by Charles R. Swindoll, Inc.

Editor in Chief: Cynthia Swindoll, President, Insight for Living
Executive Vice President: Wayne Stiles, Th.M., D.Min.,
  Dallas Theological Seminary
Content Editor: Amy L. Snedaker, B.A., English, Rhodes College
Copy Editors: Jim Craft, M.A., English, Mississippi College
  Melanie Munnell, M.A., Humanities,
  The University of Texas at Dallas
Project Coordinator, Creative Ministries: Kim Gibbs,
  Trinity Valley Community College, 1991–1993
Project Coordinator, Communications: Karen Berard, B.A.,
  Mass Communications, Texas State University-San Marcos
Proofreader: Paula McCoy, B.A., English,
  Texas A&M University-Commerce
Cover Design: Kari Pratt, B.A., Commercial Art,
  Southwestern Oklahoma State University
Production Artist: Nancy Gustine, B.F.A., Advertising Art,
  University of North Texas
Back Cover Photo: David Edmondson

Unless otherwise identified, Scripture quotations are from the *New American Standard Bible*® (NASB). Copyright © 1960, 1962, 1963, 1968, 1971, 1972, 1973, 1975, 1977, 1995 by The Lockman Foundation, La Habra, California. All rights reserved. Used by permission. (www.lockman.org)

Scripture quotations marked (MSG) are from *The Message*. Copyright © 1993, 1994, 1995, 1996, 2000, 2001, 2002 by Eugene H. Peterson. All rights reserved. Used by permission of NavPress Publishing Group.

An effort has been made to locate sources and obtain permission where necessary for the quotations used in this Bible Companion. In the event of any unintentional omission, a modification will gladly be incorporated in future printings.

ISBN: 978-1-57972-853-3
Printed in the United States of America

A Letter from Chuck

Nathaniel Hawthorne's classic novel, *The Scarlet Letter*, vividly captures a universal human gnawing—the despair of shame. In Hawthorne's tale, the young Hester Prynne has an adulterous affair with the local minister, Arthur Dimmesdale, which produces a daughter—Pearl. As a public display of her shame, Hester must wear a scarlet "A" sewn to the front of her dress. Dimmesdale, the celebrated pastor, harbors his shame privately—a torment that drives him to brand an "A" into his chest.

Adulterers no longer walk around with scarlet "A's" pinned to their chests, yet the shame that comes with such sin often sears the spirit as brutally as the letter "A" burned into Dimmesdale's flesh. But it's not just the adulterous "A" that gives birth to shame. Many carry a scarlet "A" for alcoholism, a "P" for pornography, a "D" for drug abuse, a "T" for thief, or an "H" for homosexuality.

Others through no fault of their own also feel shame. They feel the cowering shame of what has been done *to* them, such as abuse as a child and/or rape. Many feel shame due to the challenges of a disability or deformity.

Whatever the reason, if you're burdened by shame then this booklet has your name written on it. You'll meet a woman who committed adultery, but unlike Hester, she found compassion and grace from a Man who forgave and set her free from the shame that shackled her.

Would you like to meet this Man yourself and find forgiveness and freedom from your bondage of shame? Then turn the page, and let me introduce you to Him.

Chuck Swindoll

Charles R. Swindoll

Releasing the Burden of SHAME

When it comes to public shame, few people think of Jesus. If I were to ask you to list the names of twenty people you feel are deserving of shame, you'd probably not include the name Jesus Christ. I'm certainly not suggesting that He is deserving of shame, but we easily forget He experienced it.

The sinless Son of God took all our sins on Himself when He died on the cross. It was there He endured the shame of the world. Every wicked deed done by humanity, He took on Himself when He suffered and died in our place. The horror of Auschwitz, the evils of Stalin and Pol Pot and Saddam Hussein, the atrocities of Rwanda, the silent slaughter of tens of millions of aborted children, the maximum depth of each of our sinful thoughts, and the full extent of our reckless actions—all were piled on Christ at the cross. His death personified shame.

Many who have seen and felt the power of Mel Gibson's film *The Passion of the Christ* have a renewed appreciation for the depth of shame

Christ endured on our behalf during His final, agonizing hours on earth. As all of that came clear to me while watching the film, I found myself sobbing with my head in my hands.

In his volume, *The Execution of Jesus*, William Riley Wilson wrote,

> Not only was the cross the most painful of deaths, it was also considered the most debasing. The condemned man was stripped naked and left exposed in his agony, and often the Romans even denied burial to the victim, allowing his body to hang on the cross until it disintegrated. It is understandable that, according to Jewish law, anyone who was crucified was considered cursed.[1]

To be cursed is to suffer shame. Twelfth-century monk Bernard of Clairvaux described it this way:

> O sacred Head, now wounded,
> With grief and shame weighed down,
> Now scornfully surrounded
> With thorns Thine only crown;
> How pale art Thou with anguish,

With sore abuse and scorn,
How does that visage languish,
Which once was bright as morn![2]

Public Shame Explored and Examined

The old monk understood that agony and cruelty are often connected with shame. Shame runs deeper than guilt. Guilt typically remains a private affair. We learn to keep those inner indictments to ourselves, safely out of public view. But shame follows you wherever you go like a bad rap sheet. Shame straps you to your torturous past, putting everything on display. Private shame—the shame that comes from years of physical or sexual abuse, or the lonely suffering that emerges from disabilities such as speech impediments, anxiety or eating disorders, a prison sentence or time spent in a mental institution or a rehab clinic—pushes victims to the corners of the room, into the shadows of society. Shame becomes a relentless, accusing voice that whispers, "You are worthless! You don't mean anything to anyone! You're totally unworthy! You will never amount to anything! You blew it! You're finished!"

Shame penetrates deeper than embarrassment; it cuts wider than disappointment. Its scars are ugly and often seem permanent. Being the lowest form of self-hatred, shame has driven many people slumping under its burden to retreat into a sort of living death, which can ultimately end in suicide.

Shame keeps a young mother chained to her emotionally traumatic past, bruised and battered sexually by her drunken father.

Shame haunts a middle-aged woman expected by others to "move on" in her life following her husband's reckless affair and their subsequent bitter divorce.

Shame assails a teenager lost in a world of confusion and seclusion brought about by his or her inability to learn as quickly as others and compete with peers.

Shame holds back a child born with a deformity or disability from experiencing the carefree joys of recess and field trips.

Shame assaults the church leader caught in an illicit relationship with one of his parishioners and forced to confess his sin publicly.

A man I now respect and consider a friend experienced the depth of that intense shame. He was once an honored pastor with a good marriage and a fine family. But there existed a shadowy twist to his story. Eventually it came to light that he was involved sexually with one of his church members. Found out, he stood before the church and confessed his sin and felt the depth of public shame.

Years later, in a conversation he and I had about that awful period of his life, he said, "I don't know that I have words to describe the shame my family and I experienced. I found that I could negotiate my way around guilt, but I could not rationalize shame. My wife and I still look back on that dark day, calling it 'Black Sunday.'" Along with his wife and children, he felt what few people ever do—the painful alienation of public shame. To this day, tears are near the surface when that dark day is mentioned.

The binding reality of shame can't simply be sloughed off. There remains a lingering disgrace that holds us tightly in its grip.

But that bottomless despair does not have to be our lot indefinitely. The scars need not be permanent. Christ desires to meet us in those dark corners and lift us to safety by redeeming our dignity and worth. His grace is greater than our shame. Where sin abounds, grace superabounds! He becomes for us our personal shame-bearer who walks with us through those harsh, agonizing days when we feel most alone and afraid. How can He do that? Remember, He's been there. He has felt the aches of indignity and humiliation. In fact, there's no limit to the depth of shame He can see us through, because there's no limit to the grace He can supply.

Travel back with me to a first-century scene. Jesus confronts a broken and humiliated woman ensnared in the most shameful of circumstances. We are allowed to watch as He rescues her from the jagged edge of shame's powerful jaws.

An Adulteress and Her Accusers

A nameless woman took center stage in one of the most poignant scenes in all the New Testament. There, in the midst of her sin, she encountered Jesus, the Savior of the world. She assumed that her deeds done in the dark would never be known in the light. Hers was a shameful, secret sin. Then one day she came face to face with Jesus, the spotless Lamb of God, whose penetrating gaze looked squarely on her disgrace.

We are indebted to one of Jesus's original disciples, John, for including this narrative as part of his record of Christ's ministry to the broken people of Judea. Read carefully his description of this unusually delicate scene.

> Early in the morning He came again into the temple, and all the people were coming to Him; and He sat down and began to teach them. The scribes and the Pharisees brought a woman caught in adultery, and having set her in the center of the court, they said to Him, "Teacher, this woman has been caught in adultery, in the very act. Now in the Law Moses commanded us to stone such women; what then do You say?" They were saying this, testing Him, so that they might have grounds for accusing Him. But Jesus stooped down and with His finger wrote on the ground. But when they persisted in asking Him, He straightened up, and said to them, "He who is without sin among you, let him be the first to throw a stone at her." Again He stooped down and wrote on the ground. When they heard it, they began to go out one by one, beginning with the older ones, and He was left alone, and the woman, where she was, in the center of the

court. Straightening up, Jesus said to her, "Woman, where are they? Did no one condemn you?" She said, "No one, Lord." And Jesus said, "I do not condemn you, either. Go. From now on sin no more." (John 8:2–11)

You have just read one of the most remarkable dramas in the entire Bible. We can only imagine what it would have been like to have been a bug on the wall of that temple, watching it unfold.

It all began early in the morning when Jerusalem lay damp with dew. Long purple shadows fell among the temple columns. Songbirds chirped in the low-hanging trees. Several people joined in what we would call today a small-group Bible study, taught by the One who taught as no other. They had come to hear the words of the thirty-something-year-old teacher from Nazareth. He was young, but He had wisdom beyond His years. They had no idea what they would hear from Him that morning. A crowd had gathered in the temple court to hear Jesus; no doubt many spent the night on the cool ground to make certain they could sit up close. In rabbinical fashion, Jesus sat down with them as He began to teach.

Suddenly a regiment of stern-faced scribes and Pharisees interrupted Jesus, dragging a disheveled woman across the pavement and into the great hall. The people must have gasped in disbelief at the spectacle. Jesus rose to His feet and faced the self-righteous brigade of clerics and their humiliated prisoner in tow. They were the grace-killing legalists of Israel, all spit-shined and polished for another day's work of judging and criticizing others. They had come to make a public example of someone who didn't belong in their midst. Not a man, but a woman. But not just any woman . . . a lady of the night who had just been in bed with a man who wasn't her husband. They had actually caught her in the act.

The woman—never named by John or anyone else in the story—must have stood trembling like an abused dog, muzzled by fear. Her head was bowed, her hair disheveled, her clothing torn. Shame was written across her face. Her accusers planned to use her to trap Jesus. They loathed Him and His teaching and especially His growing popularity. They hated His grace most of all. Their goal was to get Him killed, whatever it took. What they were doing on this morning was all part of a diabolical plan to rid themselves and the land of the menacing prophet from Nazareth.

The religious leaders abruptly addressed Jesus. "Teacher, this woman has been caught in adultery, in the very act. Now in the Law Moses commanded us to stone such women; what then do You say?" (John 8:4–5). Interestingly, they invoked the name of Moses before they leveled the charge.

That was part of the trap. They hauled this pitiful woman in front of Jesus and a crowd of wide-eyed people, claimed the authority of Moses, and then asked sneering, "What then do You say?" British author William Barclay wrote:

> The Scribes and Pharisees were out to get some charge on which they could discredit Jesus; and here they thought they had impaled Him inescapably on the horns of a dilemma. When a difficult legal question arose, the natural and routine thing was to take it to a rabbi for a decision. So the Scribes and Pharisees approached Jesus as a rabbi.[3]

The Mishnah, Judaism's handbook of religious tradition, minces no words. It mandates that a man caught in adultery is to be strangled and placed knee-deep in dung, with a towel wrapped around his neck so the rope won't break his skin. A woman caught in the act of adultery must face public stoning. Moses had written in the Law that if the act occurred in a city, both the man and woman are to be stoned. Was this particular woman guilty? Absolutely. They apparently caught her in the very act of sexual intercourse. The Greek word translated "caught" literally means "seize" or "overtake," [4] suggesting that her accusers themselves found her in the very act of adultery and apprehended her while still in bed with her partner. But what about the man? Had he escaped? Likely not, since the religious leaders would have easily outnumbered him. My suspicions prompt me to suggest that he was a coconspirator (maybe one of them!), who had been put up to the lurid tryst beforehand. A conspiracy is not out of the question, knowing the wickedness of the accusers' hearts. The trembling woman in disarray, humiliated in front of the morning Bible study group, was nothing more than half a small piece of bait used to capture bigger game. They had Jesus in their sights. They cared nothing about the woman or her future. At that moment she meant nothing to them or to anyone else for that matter—no one except Jesus.

The unflappable young Teacher stood silently and stared, studying the entire scene. I find it remarkable that Jesus often said more in His silence than with His words. There's wisdom in remaining quiet at such crucial moments when charges are flying and tempers are flaring.

But Jesus knew the hearts of these men. He read their motive like an open book. He sensed their deliberate attempt to catch Him unprepared and snare Him with His own words.

Consider quickly the options. Had Jesus immediately agreed to the stoning, they could have accused Him of hypocrisy. A man who had been teaching the importance of compassion and forgiveness would not allow such a harsh penalty. In addition, had Jesus made that call, He could have been charged with treason. Only a Roman official could determine the verdict of death on an individual. Jesus would have had no legal authority to have her stoned to death.

On the other hand, had He simply demanded she be forgiven and set free, they would have pounced on Him for condoning sin and ignoring the Law of Moses.

Choosing neither option, according to John's narrative, "Jesus stooped down and with His finger wrote on the ground" (John 8:6). The only time in all Scripture where we're told Jesus wrote anything is here in this scene. But what did He write? There are some who believe Jesus simply scribbled in the dust as He was collecting His thoughts. Yet the Greek word translated "wrote" suggests something more.

I believe John was an eyewitness. Writing toward the end of the first century AD, he recorded that Jesus *wrote* in the sand. The Greek term John used, which the English renders as "wrote," was *katagrapho*. The last half of that word, *grapho*, is the verb "write."[5] The Greek prefix *kata* can mean "against."[6] In other words, I'm suggesting that John intended to show that Jesus wrote something in the sand that would have been incriminating to the religious leaders. Perhaps He actually did write something "against" them. Could it be that Jesus stooped and began to write out the sins of the woman's accusers in letters large enough for them and others to read? Pause and picture the scene as each accuser read his own sins written in the sand. We cannot say for sure that this is what occurred, but if it did, can you imagine their surprise?

Who or What Condemns You?

The silence was broken by the words Jesus spoke. While some ambiguity remains as to exactly what He wrote in the sand, no doubt remains about the meaning of what He said. As the scribes and Pharisees frowned and stared, Jesus rose to His feet and said to them, "He who is without sin among you, let him be the first to throw a stone at her" (John 8:7). Talk about shock! Such an incisive answer hit them like a fist in the face.

In fact, the text literally reads, "The sinless one of you, first, on her, let him cast a stone." That's awkward in English, but emphatic in Greek. In so many words, Jesus said, "The first one whom I invite to throw a stone is the sinless one! Be sure you have no sins against you. And then you're qualified to bring shame, accusation, and even death on this woman. Only make sure your hearts are pure and sinless."

An aching, awkward silence followed Christ's stinging reply. A mute void swept across the once snarling pack of junkyard dogs. What a moment!

Peter Marshall captured the scene in a vivid manner:

> Looking into their faces, Christ sees into the yesterdays that lie deep in the pools of memory and conscience. He sees into their very hearts, and that moving finger writes on . . .
>
> Idolater . . .

Liar . . .

Drunkard . . .

Murderer . . .

Adulterer . . .

There is the thud of stone after
stone falling on the pavement.
Not many of the Pharisees are left.
One by one, they creep away —
like animals — slinking into the
shadows . . . shuffling off into
the crowded streets to lose themselves in the multitudes.[7]

Can you picture it? Can you hear the dull
sound of stones hitting hard pavement? Can
you feel the humiliation of those who walked
away? The apostle John wrote, "When they heard
it, they began to go out one by one, beginning
with the older ones, and He was left alone, and
the woman, where she was, in the center of the
court" (John 8:9).

Wouldn't you love to have been a part of
the class that morning? Jesus, after dismissing
the accusers, looked directly into the eyes of
a woman full of shame, openly exposed and

17

condemned by her accusers. And if that were not enough, there she stood before the righteous Judge of the universe, guilty of adultery, having broken God's holy Law. As she met the gaze of the spotless Savior, we need to realize there has not been in the history of time a more remarkable and striking contrast of character: a woman . . . a man; a sinner . . . the sinless Son of God; the shameful adulteress . . . the Holy One of heaven. Imagine it! Two more different people never stood so close.

It is that which makes the final exchange between them so profound. It is here that grace eclipses shame.

> Straightening up, Jesus said to her, "Woman, where are they? Did no one condemn you?" She said, "No one, Lord." And Jesus said, "I do not condemn you, either. Go. From now on sin no more." (John 8:10–11)

The only person on earth qualified to condemn the woman refused to do so. Instead, He freed her. Could it be that for the first time in her life she stopped condemning herself too? That's what Jesus does for us in the humiliating blast of shame — He delivers us from self-condemnation as He sets us free.

To All Weighed Down
by Shame

At times, I wish I could wave a wand over those weighed down by shame and say, "Shame, be gone!" But it doesn't work like that. However, what Jesus did for this broken woman that morning so many centuries ago, He wants to do for you as well. It might not happen instantly, but given the opportunity to step in and bring relief (as He did with the woman that morning), Jesus can make a profound difference!

As we close this booklet on releasing the burden of shame, here are two simple statements that I'm hoping will help you in your struggle to put your painful memories and shameful thoughts behind you.

First, *those most unqualified to condemn you, will*. Count on it. Those with hearts heavier than the stones in their hands will be the first to throw them. Stay away from modern-day Pharisees, who love few things more than exposing your sin and rubbing your nose in shame. Make certain you keep plenty of distance between you and those who would throw self-righteous stones at you.

Second, *the One most qualified to condemn you, won't*. You can count on this as well. Stay close to

Him. Because by staying close to Him, you will discover that you can recover from your shame more quickly. Draw near and confess your sin to the One who is qualified to condemn but doesn't. And like the woman, you'll be able to go on with your life enjoying a new freedom and purpose for living.

In John Bunyan's *The Pilgrim's Progress*, the young character Christian walks his journey carrying a heavy burden on his back. The burden is sin—all his shameful past. The weight is bound to him with strings tight and strong. He can find no relief. Shame and disgrace along with self-condemnation weigh down on his frame. Finally, at long last, he comes to the Wicket Gate. He opens the gate and follows a narrow path which leads to the precipice. There he encounters Jesus Christ, the only One qualified to condemn him, yet He doesn't. Christian gazes across a vast chasm and sees in the distance a barren cross and, nearby, an empty tomb. While watching and meditating on the cross and the tomb, the burden that has been bound tightly to him begins to loosen. A song of freedom fills his grateful heart:

> Thus far I did come laden with
>   my sin;
> Nor could ought ease the grief that
>   I was in,

Till I came hither: What a place
is this!
Must here be the beginning of my
bliss?
Must here the Burden fall from off
my back?
Must here the strings that bound it
to me crack?
Blest Cross! Blest sepulcher! Blest
rather be
The Man that there was put to
Shame for me! [8]

What will it take to bring you to such a
defining moment? Do I make light of your sin?
Not for a moment. Your sin and mine nailed
Jesus to that cross. Our sin separated even the
Son of God from intimate fellowship with the
Father. Our failure and our shame drove spikes
into His hands and feet. Your shame and mine
cost Jesus His life. Yet the Scriptures proclaim,
"He made Him who knew no sin to be sin on our
behalf, so that we might become the righteous-
ness of God in Him" (2 Corinthians 5:21).

In other words, He took our place on that
"blest cross!" In that "blest sepulcher!" Let's
face it; there are and there will be moments
in our lives when we get "caught in the very
act." It may not be adultery but something else.

It's sin just the same. But because of Jesus we don't have to live a life of self-condemnation and debilitating shame. The Savior's words to you in your shame are the same now as they were then: "I do not condemn you, either. Go. From now on sin no more" (John 8:11). That means you're free.

If you're reading this and feeling the weight of your own shameful past or stubborn sinful ways, I invite you to come to the Savior. He's the only One perfectly qualified to judge you and condemn you, but because of what His death accomplished, He is ready to forgive and to set you free. His invitation to freedom requires your response. It isn't automatic. Being delivered from shame's shackles necessitates your coming to the precipice of the cross and acknowledging your need for Jesus. He will be there to cleanse you and make you whole.

> Are you tired? Worn out? Burned out on religion? Come to me. Get away with me and you'll recover your life. I'll show you how to take a real rest. Walk with me and work with me—watch how I do it. Learn the unforced rhythms of grace. I won't lay anything heavy or ill-fitting on you. Keep company with me and

you'll learn to live freely and lightly.
(Matthew 11:28–30 MSG)

The "unforced rhythms of grace" will truly and completely set you free. So what are you waiting for?

How to Begin a Relationship with God

The shame of past deeds — some done to us, others done by us — can cause immense pain, often far more than we'd ever imagine based on the original act. That shame threatens to cripple us emotionally, make us ineffective in the raising of our children, or harm our performance in the workplace. Thanks be to God that His grace is greater than our shame. He offers to walk with us through the dark days of shame and point the way ahead to a life that finds fulfillment and healing in His sovereign care.

Building a life released from the burden of shame depends first upon possessing a solid foundation in Jesus Christ. This comes through believing in Him as the Savior of our sins and the Lord of our lives. Without a personal relationship with Christ, developing character becomes mere preference rather than an absolute necessity. The Bible marks the path to God with four essential truths. Let's look at each marker in detail.

Our Spiritual Condition:
Totally Depraved

The first truth is rather personal. One look in the mirror of Scripture, and our human condition becomes painfully clear:

> "There is none righteous, not even one;
> There is none who understands,
> There is none who seeks for God;
> All have turned aside, together they
>   have become useless;
> There is none who does good,
> There is not even one."
>   (Romans 3:10–12)

We are all sinners through and through—totally depraved. Now, that doesn't mean we've committed every atrocity known to humankind. We're not as *bad* as we can be, just as *bad off* as we can be. Sin colors all our thoughts, motives, words, and actions.

If you've been around a while, you likely already believe it. Look around. Everything around us bears the smudge marks of our sinful nature. Despite our best efforts to create a perfect world, crime statistics continue to soar, divorce rates keep climbing, and families keep crumbling.

Something has gone terribly wrong in our society and in ourselves—something deadly. Contrary to how the world would repackage it, "me-first" living doesn't equal rugged individuality and freedom; it equals death. As Paul said in his letter to the Romans, "The wages of sin is death" (Romans 6:23)—our spiritual and physical death that comes from God's righteous judgment of our sin, along with all of the emotional and practical effects of this separation that we experience on a daily basis. This brings us to the second marker: God's character.

God's Character: Infinitely Holy

How can God judge us for a sinful state we were born into? Our total depravity is only half the answer. The other half is God's infinite holiness.

The fact that we know things are not as they should be points us to a standard of goodness beyond ourselves. Our sense of injustice in life on this side of eternity implies a perfect standard of justice beyond our reality. That standard and source is God Himself. And God's standard of holiness contrasts starkly with our sinful condition.

Scripture says that "God is Light, and in Him there is no darkness at all" (1 John 1:5). God is absolutely holy — which creates a problem for us. If He is so pure, how can we who are so impure relate to Him?

Perhaps we could try being better people, try to tilt the balance in favor of our good deeds, or seek out methods for self-improvement. Throughout history, people have attempted to live up to God's standard by keeping the Ten Commandments or living by their own code of ethics. Unfortunately, no one can come close to satisfying the demands of God's law. Romans 3:20 says, "By the works of the Law no flesh will be justified in His sight; for through the Law comes the knowledge of sin."

Our Need: A Substitute

So here we are, sinners by nature and sinners by choice, trying to pull ourselves up by our own bootstraps to attain a relationship with our holy Creator. But every time we try, we fall flat on our faces. We can't live a good enough life to make up for our sin, because God's standard isn't "good enough" — it's *perfection*. And we can't make amends for the offense our sin has created without dying for it.

Who can get us out of this mess?

If someone could live perfectly, honoring God's law, and would bear sin's death penalty for us—in our place—then we would be saved from our predicament. But is there such a person? Thankfully, yes!

Meet your substitute—*Jesus Christ*. He is the One who took death's place for you!

> [God] made [Jesus Christ] who knew no sin to be sin on our behalf, so that we might become the righteousness of God in Him. (2 Corinthians 5:21)

God's Provision: A Savior

God rescued us by sending His Son, Jesus, to die on the cross for our sins (1 John 4:9–10). Jesus was fully human and fully divine (John 1:1, 18), a truth that ensures His understanding of our weaknesses, His power to forgive, and His ability to bridge the gap between God and us (Romans 5:6–11). In short, we are "justified as a gift by His grace through the redemption which is in Christ Jesus" (Romans 3:24). Two words in this verse bear further explanation: *justified* and *redemption*.

Justification is God's act of mercy, in which He declares righteous the believing sinners while we are still in our sinning state. Justification doesn't mean that God *makes* us righteous, so that we never sin again, rather that He *declares* us righteous—much like a judge pardons a guilty criminal. Because Jesus took our sin upon Himself and suffered our judgment on the cross, God forgives our debt and proclaims us PARDONED.

Redemption is Christ's act of paying the complete price to release us from sin's bondage. God sent His Son to bear His wrath for all of our sins—past, present, and future (Romans 3:24–26; 2 Corinthians 5:21). In humble obedience, Christ willingly endured the shame of the cross for our sake (Mark 10:45; Romans 5:6–8; Philippians 2:8). Christ's death satisfied God's righteous demands. He no longer holds our sins against us, because His own Son paid the penalty for them. We are freed from the slave market of sin, never to be enslaved again!

Placing Your Faith in Christ

These four truths describe how God has provided a way to Himself through Jesus Christ.

Because the price has been paid in full by God, we must respond to His free gift of eternal life in total faith and confidence in Him to save us. We must step forward into the relationship with God that He has prepared for us — not by doing good works or by being a good person but by coming to Him just as we are and accepting His justification and redemption by faith.

> For by grace you have been saved through faith; and that not of your-selves, it is the gift of God; not as a result of works, so that no one may boast. (Ephesians 2:8–9)

We accept God's gift of salvation simply by placing our faith in Christ alone for the forgiveness of our sins. Would you like to enter a relationship with your Creator by trusting in Christ as your Savior? If so, here's a simple prayer you can use to express your faith:

> *Dear God,*
>
> *I know that my sin has put a barrier between You and me. Thank You for sending Your Son, Jesus, to die in my place. I trust in Jesus alone to forgive my sins, and I accept His gift of eternal life. I ask Jesus to be my personal Savior*

*and the Lord of my life. Thank You. In
Jesus's name, amen.*

If you've prayed this prayer or one like it and you wish to find out more about knowing God and His plan for you in the Bible, contact us at Insight for Living. Our contact information is on the following pages.

We Are Here for You

If you desire to find out more about knowing God and His plan for you in the Bible, contact us. Insight for Living provides staff pastors who are available for free written correspondence or phone consultation. These seminary-trained and seasoned counselors have years of experience and are well-qualified guides for your spiritual journey.

Please feel welcome to contact your regional Pastoral Ministries by using the information below:

United States

Insight for Living
Pastoral Ministries
Post Office Box 269000
Plano, Texas 75026-9000
USA
972-473-5097, Monday through Friday,
8:00 a.m. – 5:00 p.m. Central time
www.insight.org/contactapastor

Canada

Insight for Living Canada
Pastoral Ministries
Post Office Box 2510
Vancouver, BC V6B 3W7
CANADA
1-800-663-7639
info@insightforliving.ca

Australia, New Zealand, and South Pacific

Insight for Living Australia
Pastoral Care
Post Office Box 443
Boronia, VIC 3155
AUSTRALIA
1 300 467 444

United Kingdom and Europe

Insight for Living United Kingdom
PO Box 553
Dorking
RH4 9EU
UNITED KINGDOM
0800 915 9364
pastoralcare@insightforliving.org.uk

Endnotes

1. William Riley Wilson, *The Execution of Jesus: A Judicial, Literary and Historical Investigation* (New York: Simon & Schuster, 1970), 152.

2. Bernard of Clairvaux, "O Sacred Head, Now Wounded" (Nashville: Word, Music/Integrity Music, 1997), 316.

3. William Barclay, *The Gospel of John*, rev. ed. (Louisville, Ky.: Westminster John Knox Press, 1975), 2:1–2. Used by permission.

4. Frederick William Danker, ed., *A Greek-English Lexicon of the New Testament and Other Early Christian Literature*, 3d ed. (Chicago: University of Chicago Press, 2000), 520.

5. Danker, ed., *A Greek-English Lexicon of the New Testament and Other Early Christian Literature*, 207.

6. Danker, ed., *A Greek-English Lexicon of the New Testament and Other Early Christian Literature*, 511.

7. Catherine Marshall, *A Man Called Peter: The Story of Peter Marshall* (Grand Rapids: Chosen Books, a division of Baker Publishing Group, 1949), 314. Used by permission.

8. John Bunyan, *Pilgrim's Progress* (Uhrichsville, Oh.: Barbour Books, an imprint of Barbour Publishing), 36. Used by permission.

Ordering Information

If you would like to order additional booklets or request other products, please contact the office that serves you.

United States
Insight for Living
Post Office Box 269000
Plano, Texas 75026-9000
USA
1-800-772-8888
(Monday through Friday,
7:00 a.m.–7:00 p.m. Central time)
www.insight.org
www.insightworld.org

Canada
Insight for Living Canada
Post Office Box 2510
Vancouver, BC V6B 3W7
CANADA
1-800-663-7639
www.insightforliving.ca

Australia, New Zealand, and South Pacific

Insight for Living Australia

Post Office Box 443

Boronia, VIC 3155

AUSTRALIA

1 300 467 444

www.insight.asn.au

United Kingdom and Europe

Insight for Living United Kingdom

PO Box 553

Dorking

RH4 9EU

UNITED KINGDOM

0800 915 9364

www.insightforliving.org.uk

Other International Locations

International constituents may contact
the U.S. office through our Web site
(www.insightworld.org), mail queries, or
by calling +1-972-473-5136.